BEYOND THE CROSS

The Christ Collection

Joseph Raffa

Beyond the Cross – The Christ Collection

Author: Joseph Raffa

Editor: Teena Raffa-Mulligan

First published in 1999 by Harmony House Press

This edition published in 2014 by Teena Raffa-Mulligan

ISBN 978-0-9872276-5-2

Printed by CreateSpace, an Amazon.com company
Available from CreateSpace.com, Amazon.com and other
retail outlets

CONTENTS

JOSEPH'S LEGACY

JOSEPH RAFFA WAS no ordinary man. The sparkle in his eyes meant more than playful intent. It spoke of something special inside him... another-worldly knowledge that left him in the world but not of it.

Joe tells his own story at the beginning of this book. But there are those of us, blessed by knowing him, who would like to share a little about the man who touched us in so many ways.

His was a life of simplicity. Disinterested in the material world and its values, he preferred to enjoy the treats that nature offered. A beautiful sunset, the wind on his face, the trees that surrounded his home and the ocean he visited daily. While his devoted wife Barbara was alive, theirs was a home of warmth, welcome, meaningful discussion and Barbara's delicious cooking.

In his early twenties, after much inner turmoil and conflict, Joe had an epiphany, an inner illumination which permanently altered the way he viewed life right up until his passing. The legacy of this event led to the prolific writing of his inner experiences, insights, visions and understandings. Prompted by urgings in the early hours of the morning, he went obediently to his typewriter and over many years, the collection of writings culminated into a small library.

Those of us who were privy to those writings were inspired by what he had to say and often pressed him to publish them. Disinterested in such things, he had a better idea. He had fathered a daughter and fellow soul traveller who would turn out to be the second part of this partnership. Teena, an author herself, intuitively felt it was her role to take such work to the public. This is the first offering in her labour of love ... Beyond the Cross.

Gypsy Wulff
May 2012

BY WAY OF EXPLANATION

YEARS AGO, WHEN I set off in search of God, I was a dedicated, discontented atheist. I won't dwell on the reasons that urged me towards God but it was very important to me at the time. It seemed like the only worthwhile thing left in life to do. Work, marriage, family, car and a home had been taken care of or would be in time.

In my days of non-belief, science was the only authority that mattered to me. From this I expected the answers that would be the solution to the riddles of life and the universe, of the how, why and whereto of everything. Many a vigorous verbal battle have I fought with Jehovah's Witnesses or others of their ilk who knocked on my door to discuss religion. They never tired of coming, their enthusiasm reinforced with the back-up authority of The Holy Bible in their hands. Evolution and science versus religious scriptures. Oh, how the words and explanations flew back and forth. But all to no avail. We went our separate ways, each securely anchored in different standpoints. And, no doubt, life was the usual mix of troubles and enjoyment regardless of the adopted standing.

An atheistic background is an unusual one to have when one goes in search of God. But that's the way it was then and perhaps part of the fault lies in the church traditions of the time, with Latin language and the constant quote, quote, quote from the good book. I didn't have the patience to listen to the same record, played over and over without variation to the basic theme. Too much of this can dull the mind and drive a young person elsewhere in the search for something worthwhile. So the Bible and those who figured prominently in its pages, including Jesus, faded from my mind and I carried on accordingly. Science and the edicts of science took over.

But there are different ways of presenting spiritual truths. These can even be offered in a philosophical or scientific context. And with the possibility of verification from within, not at the end of a microscope or telescope or with the need of long years of university study. With this kind of offering, what could a young lad do but have a go? Suffice it to say, after a long, wearing year of application with the methods, meditation and reflection that appealed to me, what should surprisingly drop into my life, in that first blissful moment of discovery, but the very God the prophets of the Bible spoke of, the Allah of Mohammed, the longed for Nirvana of the Buddhists.

Atheism was consigned to the dustbin of my personal history and life opened out on a broader and deeper front. Now, I had something substantial to fall back on, even to use as a basis for constructive discussion. When the opportunity came to speak, I spoke, not in the language of the past but in words that were suitable in the present. When the urge to write moved me, I wrote, using the language that flowed from within.

Spiritual development continued for many years and in this time, neither the Bible nor Christ were significant, neither in my writings, nor in my thoughts. The Bible I leave to those who are interested — to historians, scholars and the like — but Christ and aspects of His life began to intrude recently, after many years on the pathway of realisation. With the opening out of the inner spiritual content I began to have a deeper appreciation of the man, His life and His role in the spiritual awakening of Mankind.

Visions and insights on various aspects of His life began to arise unbidden. Not all at once but spread over a period of time. They were interesting, compellingly clear and presented in such a manner that I did not question their authenticity.

Initially, these did not move me to write about this unusual man. This was to come later when odd scenes would open out, words begin to form, leading to a poem, prose, or even a piece appropriate for Easter or Christmas. Some of these have been published in various community newspapers.

At the times of these compelling visions, scenes would open out so clearly they were like vistas of real life, vignettes of times gone by, enclosed and holding my attention. Invariably, excitement would follow and a restlessness to reach for pen and paper to record the movement of thought that followed in the wake of these happenings. One after the other they accumulated.

It wasn't something I would have chosen to write about. The Bible, the life of Christ — this wasn't how my writing had been developing. Yet, here He was, as large as life, insisting on dropping in from time to time and encouraging in the process a written collection with Christ as the central theme and as an example for people to listen to and to learn from.

And just in case I wasn't a willing instrument, I was served notice, via an informing intuition, that I would be called on to give some support in this direction. Well, an intuition is one thing but the reality only becomes clear as it proceeds to unfold. And unfold it did, with a developing theme of articles and prose.

So, the young man who was an atheist for a time, who cared not to read the Bible or take much notice of Christ and His life, found himself not only anchored in God but also writing pieces extolling the virtues, the wisdom and the love expressed by that super, spiritual being of long ago. And doing it as though it was a normal, acceptable thing to do.

Now, writing to me is neither a business nor a profession. I write what I do because waves of energy, translating into themes and words, move me to do so. When it begins, I feel like I have been cast adrift at the mercy of wind and waves. I don't know where I'm going nor what will follow. Over the years, I have amassed quite a collection of pieces, have had one small book published (not successful in sales) and many letters printed in the various newspapers.

My writings are stacked — disorganised, many not dated — in a back room, on top of an old radiogram and in my bookcase. Being lazy and not methodical I have not kept a tidy record of what I have done. As a result, it is sometimes difficult to quickly find what I want and if I do, where are the copies? Who knows? Somewhere in one of the stacks of typed paper.

This changed somewhat a short time ago at the bidding of another wave of persistent energy. So I bought a number of files and set to and put together related pieces — a Fremantle section, letters, spiritual pieces and what I call my Christ collection. The next job was to put on computer discs what had only been typed. So far, so good. It was slowly coming together. The first wave of energy passed. The spiritual section and letters had been mainly dealt with. Next, I had set my sight on the Fremantle section — not too much work to that one. But something decreed otherwise.

Friday afternoon, January, it was hot, damned hot. The vegetable garden was gasping for water. I decided on hand watering to give it a quick splash. About half-way through another wave of energy intruded and impatience arose to leave it and go to the computer. The Christ collection came forcefully to mind. It wouldn't leave me in peace.

Well, I insisted on finishing the watering but I hurried through, then inside to sit at my computer. Out came the Christ collection and into the computer I typed the pieces that had not yet been recorded on disc. I'm slow and one or two pieces in a session is all I can manage but by Sunday dinner it was over. I turned off the computer, covered it up for protection as usual and turned to leave the room.

Then suddenly, a deep — very deep — calmness settled over me, deeper than I'd ever known before. It was such a contrast to all the hassles, tiredness and go, go, go of arranging and indexing my writings or of anything else I do. It was so persistent and unusual in its conscious impact that it puzzled me somewhat. I felt like a man who had been called on to do an exacting and difficult task (that's what writing of this kind and computer work is for me), that I'd given it my best shot regardless of my feelings, done it as well as I could and now my part was over.

The calmness I experienced left me on a heightened plateau of quietness both of mood and reason for a time. I realised it would go eventually and that the hustle and bustle of living in time and mind would swing back in again. But, for a while it was there, strange and different and that was the way of it.

Now the Christ collection is ready for whatever we can do with it. Time will show whether it has any value beyond the ordinary and whether a higher purpose moved me to write it as I did, a step at a time until it was completed.

Joseph Raffa.
January 28, 1992

1

THE CHRIST WALKED THIS WAY

OUT OF THE silence He came, out of that great love that knows not beginning or end, on a mission of mercy. He walked amongst evil, a shining star of truth, radiant with the lustre of the Strangeness. And oh, how He talked in parables of matchless beauty.

In simplicity He walked, unaided by human hands. His trust lay, not in the social tides of the day, nor in the traditional dogmas of the church of His time, but in that Timeless Tide that dwells where humans cannot go and remain human. With the God of Love He supped in timeless splendour. And when the cross reared its stark and threatening shape across the troubled landscape, unflinching and unyielding He hung there, naked and crucified.

Held there, not only by iron nails hammered deep through feeble flesh but by the tremendous strength of an immeasurable love; a human symbol of a love that defied the ravages and evil grasp of a particularly brutal time.

And then came the unbelievable — the mysterious resurrection when the Sunshine of Truth briefly walked and talked again in that very same body that had lain so deathly still. Pierced by a spear thrust through and through, and finally left for dead in a cold and lonely cave nearby.

But the power of a Great Love moved to reclaim its blessed son in fulfilment of a promise made —He arose, He walked, He talked, and those who saw, marvelled in wonder.

Then, like a phantom will-o'-the wisp, He was gone. Physically gone, perhaps for good, leaving a mystery for people to talk and to think about; and a lesson in love for all to learn from and to reach out for, if they too, could only leave this home in the vale of time and travel the timeless way to that Strangeness that possessed him so.

2

LOVE PASSED THIS WAY AND LEFT ITS CALLING CARD

WHAT A BEAUTIFUL person He was, walking quietly there; Godlike in human form beside the sea of Galilee. He dwelt in peace and timeless serenity. His eyes reflected the wisdom of the universe and sparkled with the light of love. The fresh wind from the sea rippled His robe and His sandalled feet left imprints on the sandy shore.

He called to the fishermen working there. Soft the voice, yet authority reigned. He called them away to another calling. At the sound of His voice they looked around, then back to the sea, to the boats and the nets. Glances they cast from one to another, uncertain, unsure of this new calling. The ways of the old whispered fresh with the wind, surged in the sea where the fish swam freely.

Again He beckoned. "Why do you pause? The world awaits us. Come. Let us go on a mission of peace, with a message of love."

As the fresh wind stirred the sea and the boats, this fateful group with Him at the helm walked away from the shore and over the hills.

Now the footsteps are lost in the mists of time, the faces gone and the voices stilled. But He still stands, nailed to the cross. Courage unbroken, spirit unbowed. Where others fled, He stood alone — unyielding — this servant of love. His sacrifice a call to the human race, His cross a symbol of the highest love, His life a reflection of divine intent, His death — a pause.

Then He rose anew from His grave in a cave, walked again with those who shared His life; talked, then left, His life's work done. Mission accomplished — in peace — and stamped with love.

3

THE GREATEST MYSTERY

I**T WOULD SEEM** the greatest mystery in human history is the mystery of Jesus Christ. Volumes have been written for and against many aspects of His life and today, come Easter or Christmas, controversy surfaces about the nature of the man and the recorded events of His life.

We who live ordinary lives find the reports of healing, the miracles and the resurrection difficult, even impossible to understand. The inspiration in His words, the spiritual outpouring and the quality of His life are acknowledged by the sensitively attuned.

Yet the sombre events that took place on

that cross almost two thousand years ago still have the power to move people to tears and defy the capacity of unenlightened intellects to understand. What is there then, to understand in intellectual terms? He came, He passed through and He conquered by the power of a great love for Mankind, by the inspiration of His life and His words. For a human outlet the spiritual outpouring was immense and such was its force that it spread from its centre in this man to flow around the world.

He stands as an example of what humans must aspire to. Not towards unusual effects that sometimes accompany spiritual persons of this magnitude but towards spiritual discovery and union with this strange nature we call God. The encouragement He gave that such does indeed exist, and that it is the greatest blessing that humans can share, was the most important legacy He left the human race.

4

THERE IS STILL MYSTERY

WE CANNOT UNDERSTAND beings different from ourselves. We are too conditioned by our human experience, by reason and by our normal level of understanding. What we see, know and accept are a product of what we are.

Our investigations of God, life and the universe fall within this circle of our limited standpoint — the human one. We may take what we consider to be an impersonal or unbiased approach, cross-checking and testing, logically or experimentally, in our efforts to determine the truth we seek but in the final analysis, we can only arrive at conclusions that make sense to us.

This is fundamental in our approach to learning. We begin with, we operate by and at the end we are still within the confines of the human level of understanding. It is through this that we learn what we do and we cannot be any different unless in some way this basic level undergoes some kind of a boosting impulse that lifts it out of its accustomed level and onto a super level of understanding. In a sense this sounds contradictory, for in those moments when this takes place, the ordinary in fact comes to a complete end, ceases to function and so a higher level can flood through without distortion or interference.

Ordinary human understanding will always interpret phenomena, history and present events from this standing, deeply convinced it has the capacity to see clearly and understand fully the nature of what is taking place. But what manifests on the surface, the events that flow through the frames of space and time, are a consequence of a creative arisal taking place on levels outside our conscious perception.

Human history, reviewed from the outside, is seemingly a response to stimuli and challenges, an expression of desires and intentions, ideas and purposes. To those who take a surface view, no matter how analytical or logical, there appears to be only the human component involved as we know it, the other life forms we come into contact with, the environment and the forces of nature.

In the normal course, we do not have any evidence of anything we could call supernatural or that we cannot explain by the light of human reason. After years of applied investigation we have our explanations as to why things happen as they do, why the universe and life are here and, in our way, we are comfortable with the conclusions arrived at.

But then, along came this upstart, this person who upset our rational applecart and threatened by His actions and the events of His life to tip the apples of customary experience and acquired knowledge out of their accepted order and scatter them in the uncertain direction of not being explainable or understood. I refer to Jesus Christ.

A far greater mystery is the nature of what we humans refer to as God and perhaps the discovery of this helps to deepen the understanding of a man such as Jesus. God, we find rather inaccessible, so much so that in our framework of logical explanations it is discarded by most (scientists and laypeople) as being of little or no consequence in our understanding of history or universal phenomena.

That is one way of dealing with the matter. With that of Jesus, we still have problems after two thousand years of investigation and analytical examination. Scholars and historians argue points of interpretation even when they have access to the same written records. But there is something about the man, His coming and the events of His life that disturbs us deeply.

He defies conventional behaviour and the natural order of things as we know them. He doesn't fit our preconceived notions of what human behaviour should be. If the reports are true, even in some of the details and not all, something unusual, that cannot be explained in logical thought or scientific terms was manifesting in the life of this man. So difficult in fact to understand, that perhaps it is better to dismiss it altogether and not tax our minds or weary ourselves by trying the impossible — to put rational clothes on Jesus.

There is only one great mystery of consequence — the mystery of God. From this flows all the things we wonder at — life, the universe, human history and above all, the advent of an expression like Jesus. There have been others, many others who came from the same source to help and inspire Mankind, but somehow, in Jesus, it would seem from the reports we have that a dimension of unusual happenings was added as well.

This is not to say that there have not been others with unusual powers, only that He was thrust to the forefront of the human stage to take the brunt of human aggressiveness and the reactions from deeply entrenched ignorance and long established social and religious attitudes.

So the human microscope focuses with greater intensity on this man, with debate and contention surfacing from time to time and disagreement the consequence of human effort to find answers that satisfy. And perhaps this will continue because we miss the main point of His coming.

Not the miracles and the resurrection but the overall quality of His life and the insistent importance given to the existence of God and the need for humans to surrender the self, to discover and make this nature the foundation of our day by day approach to life. His life demonstrated in every way the reality to Him of this nature and more. He was to show that in service to Mankind. Torture, even death on the cross was preferable to a denial of what He represented and knew to be true.

And this is where our difficulties lie. Our approach is intellectual. We have no discovery, no direct evidence of the existence of God, of its nature and interaction with the human expression as something ongoing day by day. We fall back on faith or belief and we walk about in circles, going from reason to reason, explanation to explanation and still at the end, there He is, transfixed on the cross, that bloody crown of thorns on His head, arms extended, hands nailed to the crossbeam, rose vines wrapped around His arms to keep him securely in position. Defying us to understand Him, His life or the God He so glowingly spoke of.

5

A NAME ETCHED IN HISTORY

CHRIST STORMED THROUGH Judea and Galilee and, in a few short years, stirred up such ferment in the way He conducted His missionary life that His name and deeds have become etched in the historical movement of Mankind's consciousness. So much so that even today He is revered by millions throughout the world.

All this from a small beginning in a barren (mostly) desert backyard of a place that no one would care about if it hadn't come to be important to the Western world and to the Jewish and Arab people who live there. It was then of somewhat strategic importance and conquering armies from East and West took turns laying claim to the area.

Somehow, because of this man and those who zealously spread His message, where He was born, where He died on the cross, His burial place and the extent of His ministry have become the focus of fervent adulation by devout Christians.

How is it that one man could initiate such a hurricane of religious change across the world? The old gods were swept aside to be replaced by the concept of One God. Idolatry was replaced with the worship of a God of light and love — a being without form or shape — something to be contacted in hallowed moments of prayerful contemplation. Living rightly according to God's laws was enthusiastically encouraged and this man who proclaimed a new way of living settled in the hearts of millions and became their inspiration.

And in a way He is with us still. Religious days are celebrated by the faithful, each according to tradition. There are churches scattered the world over with a distinguishing cross somewhere on or in the buildings. Libraries contain sections with books on His life and from time to time, controversy surfaces in the media on some aspect of His life. Who was He? What was His purpose? Were the miracles for real?

Interpretations abound as the human reason stretches every which way to understand those momentous events and the tremendous growth of the churches that followed in His name.

It was a most unusual performance and one that confounds the rational mind. Perhaps this man did have a divine backup as He claimed. After all, a divine nature is something the rational mind can't get its inquisitive nose into. What a combination that would be — the divine and the human, dwelling in loving harmony. What kind of harvest would that produce on this brawling, bruising, mixed up planet? Would it herald the end of violence and selfishness, of the divisions Mankind has raised? Would starvation be quickly dealt with and all the other kinds of actions that degrade what should be the fair and gentle face of Mankind?

I suppose Christ had the answer to that and He considered it so important He refused to compromise His standing when His time came. So, He faced the torture, the crucifixion, the taunts and all else the misunderstanding ones subjected him to. And He came up trumps. He did what He had to do — did it in style, perhaps with a sense of showmanship. It was, after all, an ingenious idea, the resurrection. It guaranteed an historical immortality.

After all these years, His light still shines down to us. When in need, knock, and in some way, He'll be there. It doesn't matter who you are, what your life has been. If the need is deep and the asking sincere, the response will come. What moved him then, what inspired him to go to the cross, is with us now. It's closer than we know, waiting for us to return. This kind of love knows no boundaries. And should the divine enfold you, just for a moment, you will have joined that hallowed nature Christ spoke about when He said, "I and my Father are One."

6

ONE NEEDS TO BE ONLY
DEEPLY HUMAN

THERE ARE PEOPLE who are Christian, and those who are not Christian; who are unbelievers, agnostics and of other faiths. But does one need to be a declared Christian to appreciate the value and importance of what happened almost two thousand years ago? Surely it is enough to be human, to share the human experience and to be sensitive in matters spiritual.

The darkness of human living was rent asunder by the coming of this man; a chasm forged through the darkness by a light of spiritual intensity. Those who lived on the level of the darkness were fascinated, even overwhelmed by the arrival of the light. The mind fails to understand, to appreciate the significance. Many feel He was merely an historical figure of exemplary character, expounding His own religious philosophy — and even cast doubt on the authenticity of the miracles He performed.

But, if we are capable of listening inwardly — of going beyond the words and the deeds — behind this man a most unusual nature expressed its intentions. It offered evidence — in the way He lived, in His commanding presence and manner, and above all, in His stoic willingness to face His fate on the cross, with the consequent resurrection — that there does indeed exist something strange, other than the human life we know, other than the natural order of things to which we are accustomed. And that, within the life we are, we can come to realise this, and likewise share in its nature and enjoy thereby the bounty of its goodness, and flourish accordingly.

7

A TRUE CHRISTIAN HAS NOUGHT TO FEAR

THE ESTABLISHED CHRISTIAN religions see the new age movements as a threat to the traditional religious approach. Yet Christ, the foundation of the Christian movement was perhaps the greatest of the new-agers — a social and religious revolutionary who defied the traditional moulds of the day. He brought a new approach to life. In a time of violence, of conquest by the sword, He advocated love, even towards enemies, and social justice founded on the nature of God.

His words were more than ideas produced by intellectual capacity. They were the direct expression of the basic values, the spirituality that was alive and active to an exceptional degree in a human being. What He offered, in its purest form above the words He used, even beyond the life that flowed from it, is what all new-agers are groping towards. Christ was united with that something more, that special significance posed by life that people yearn for in their hearts yet cannot realise with their minds. Call it God as most do. It matters not.

The longing for a sustainable basis in living, for a support that never fails, for a means that brings an end to violence, injustice, exploitation, all the wrongs evident world-wide is a powerful one embedded deep somewhere in the nature of the sensitive. People do not lightly step off in the search for God. The mind expects great things of this nature — returns that will make them happier, clearer, integrated human beings. In every way they expect to flourish from this meeting with this mysterious nature.

It is held to be the greatest of human aspirations. Some give their all — possessions, financial security, family relationships, nationality, the self they are — to be with it completely, to serve their fellow human beings and to further the cause of universal enlightenment.

Christ was such as this. That's why His coming shines out like a blazing beacon in the darkness of human living, why the events of His life and His words still endure as an inspiration today.

People are different in their approach. Styles and language change. All universal truths are constant. The means of expression are as variable as the weather. Behind the words, the styles of expression, lies that which is beyond the word. Behind the embellishments, the methods, the ways that people love to identify with, lies that which is discovered only when every covering aspect projected by the mind ceases to function. This is what Christ offered, what His life was an example of. Discover God first — then live. Discover God first — then love. Discover — that is paramount.

Without discovery how can we function from the spiritual level? We are dead inwardly. We have no truth. Our nature in its outward flow is stunted. We draw no vital sustenance. We degenerate and decay. There is nothing going for us to counterbalance the darkening effects of the mind.

The self becomes paramount. Reason is

twisted to serve the self. Means are devised to protect the self. Armies are raised; ideas, organisations, everything flows around the self and its extensions. Suspicions, concerns, anxieties, uncertainties abound. We are in disarray going in different directions without a universal directive at the helm of human affairs. We do our best but we flounder in a morass of our own making. Some are lucky and life leaves them alone in a quiet corner of the world. But many are not.

Hence what is called the new age movement. A stirring to something new, a new approach to what has always been with us. There is a freshness about a new movement, an exciting energy, particularly about movements that are bent on spiritual discovery. People are drawn together by a common interest, eager to talk about their heart's desire, eager to share experiences, hopes, unusual happenings. They encourage each other.

The true Christian has nought to fear from anyone. Such a person is securely anchored in God, is in fact a constantly new expression in living — would be a new-ager of a kind, advocating and living discovery, not through the written and spoken word, not by traditional observance, but through union, togetherness without distinction with God.

Observe the birth and then the growth of a child. Years pass before it matures physically, emotionally and mentally. Spiritual maturity takes longer. People will wander many highways and byways in their search for God, in their need for something better than what they have. They will find this when they return to their spiritual heartland. These are the new-agers wherever they appear. The social climate they pass through will only welcome them when it is already a new age climate or moving towards it. Otherwise, rejection is their lot as indeed it was with Christ.

8

A CHOICE OF KINGS

IN THE WAY we humans arrange our living there are many divisions, many classifications. We have royalty, the 'blue bloods' and the upper crust; and we have servants and the supposedly lowly. Of the royalty — the upper class — there are kings of various kinds.

Some come from a long line of tradition reaching back through centuries of time. Well established is the lineage, and these people command positions of privilege, power and wealth. They own estates, crown jewels. They control servants and workers and wherever they go the red carpet treatment awaits them. National heads greet their arrival and crowds assemble to welcome them. They rarely know hardship or want and theirs is a kingdom of material and financial security.

There are other kinds of kings who control economic estates, amass great wealth and power. They are driven around in expensive cars, travel in fast-flying jet 'planes, and often they own sea craft that are opulent in outfitting and superbly designed.

Their kingdom is an economic one and they, too, are courted world-wide. Their investments and business expertise are avidly sought and the world delights in their coming, for they bring economic abundance and material well-being. Want and security rarely trouble these kings and their security, in matters of finance, is well established.

At some time in our past there arose a different kind of king, not by human decree or social tradition; who came, not dressed in fine clothes, nor blessed with material wealth. From a humble beginning He had His start. And in His lifetime neither expensive clothes, holdings of land, nor the trappings of wealth were collected. His kingdom was by divine decree, and He ruled by inspiration and with the highest understanding.

Love was His throne throughout His short

life here, and His sceptre was one of wisdom. Understanding and compassion flowed effortlessly out of His nature. And what He dispensed in spiritual value, neither favour nor payment He accepted in return. He gave — and gave freely without charge. And when He travelled, when not on foot, why, on the back of a donkey He journeyed.

Is this, then, the true measure of greatness? Humility of such depth? Not in pomp or ceremony did He come, nor live that way. But simply, directly, moved by the power of a great love. And so He faced all the obstacles that came His way. The ill-treatment, the abuse, whatever devilish minds could devise. And He won through in flying colours.

Now He stands without peer, foremost amongst human endeavours. And one might add, when royal kings and financial emperors are forgotten, still He will be revered and remembered. For such people are rare jewels, and they shine out like lighthouses when seas are stormy and the nights darkly hide dangerous shoals.

The light He reflected is our lighthouse, shining through the gloom of our daily living and lighting our way to another world, to a different kind of living. We should aspire to such as He possessed, rather than the transitory wealth and positions owned by these other kings we know.

9

THE WAY WE CELEBRATE CHRISTMAS

WE HAVE OUR way of celebrating Christmas. The stores and shops are overflowing with goods. There is such a variety to choose from. Toys galore, so much food, coloured lights and Christmas trees, fancy decorations and music playing. Christmas carols are back again.

How different conditions are today from two thousand years ago. There, where Christ lived, the land was mostly barren desert. Here we have our forests and modern cities. We travel by motor transport, train, ship or plane.

Back then people travelled on foot, on

horse or by mule. Yet, in that arid land with its scattering of vineyards and olive groves, with an oasis here and there, a man emerged to make an impact of great spiritual consequence.

Into this land he came like a tempest from the unknown bringing a new message of love, compassion and mercy.

He walked sandy pathways on sandalled feet. His eyes gazed out on a hostile, troubled world. Aggression and repression were rife and the reality of a God of love was unknown.

He challenged every idol of the day — religious, political, social and moral. He appealed to the hearts and minds of the downtrodden and the poor. They gathered to hear Him speak.

In His time, the fancy decorations and celebration of Christmas were non-existent. His mind and life were set on the expression of higher values. His celebration was the joy of service, of giving the self to lift mankind out of the doldrums of decay into the freedom of discovery and union with the God of which He spoke.

He brought a harvest of spiritual abundance to a people devoid of spiritual value.

On the 25th of December we celebrate His life with an overload of everything that has come to mean a merry Christmas for us. We rush here and there and spend what we can afford. We may even donate a little to others less fortunate to reassure ourselves of the true meaning of Christmas.

But human nature hasn't changed much in two thousand years in spite of remembrance and celebrations year after year. Violence stalks the Earth, war breaks out and nations rely on armed might, not on peace and goodwill.

We've yet to learn the way of peace or how to express the love that was an essential part of His expression. It would seem then, that His coming brought little change for the better.

Still, my toast on Christmas goes to this man who stood head and shoulders above His contemporaries, who showed the meaning of a life simply, courageously and truthfully lived, who showed the way of love and compassion. His life pointed clearly towards the existence of that strange nature people worship as God and He lived His life unyieldingly in compliance to a higher directive even though in the end, it took Him to great suffering and death on the cross.

For all this, Christmas is deserving of quiet celebration and contemplation.

10

A CHRISTMAS CONTRAST

NOWADAYS IT WOULD SEEM that the enjoyment of Christmas is measured by an overload of fine foods, fancy boxes of chocolates, decorated bottles of wine and all the paraphernalia and preparations that go with this very special time. Christmas, without money to spend, without presents galore, without this kind of celebration, would be considered dark and gloomy – a very unhappy time indeed.

We are so imbued with this idea of what Christmas should be that to celebrate otherwise, in a quiet, contemplative way, would be a great let-down, not only for grownups but more particularly for children, who now await this time of giving and receiving presents with great anticipation. It seems we have created a monster that just keeps growing and growing, year after year and the success or otherwise of Christmas is measured by the quality and quantity of goods in the supermarkets and on the total value of money spent. The more, the merrier.

How then should we celebrate Christmas, this time of remembrance of a great love that led eventually to the highest sacrifice? With joy in our hearts? With a fresh perception of the importance of this example in living? With a deep appreciation of the living process and heartfelt thanks to the creative power that made it all possible?

And also for making it possible for humans to share this great love, this mystery nature, in wonderful moments of discovery; of sheer enchantment, that melt away the harsh, grasping tendency of the mind to hold fast to tinsel and outer show, to the fun of the fair approach we have to Christmas. To the razzle and dazzle of celebrations, to the rush, rush, rush to spend and stock up what is mostly not needed anyway, and which only serves to convince people that good times or important events are only so if they apply themselves in such an extravagant fashion. We can surely celebrate in a much more meaningful way.

11

A CHRISTMAS REFLECTION

AT CHRISTMAS THE thoughts of devout Christians turn back to the events that unfolded almost two thousand years ago. They will not only celebrate the birth of a man, a prophet, a messiah and a religious leader of outstanding qualities but also the remarkable texture of His life. His birth gave little indication of the extraordinary nature of what was to follow nor of how He was to develop into such a spiritual colossus.

From its seeds in this birth, a flowering of incredible beauty came to full bloom in an example of love, wisdom and understanding unparalleled in its expression. He wandered sandy pathways in that barren, desert land giving out His inspired message of love. Such a contrast to the aggressive displays of the time. His offering was one of peace to a strife-torn area. Peace and love. Not carnal love but spiritual love, that rare quality that flows from the meeting between God and humans.

But few there were who could respond to such a high calling and fewer still who could understand. The forces of ignorance, fear and concern for established traditions and authority rallied to crush the living flame of truth that brightly burned whenever He spoke.

There was no way though that this spiritual outpouring could be checked by the acts of desperate men. Neither torture nor the cross could halt or obliterate this man's destiny or His offering to a blighted Mankind.

We celebrate soon in recognition of those qualities and the values He represented. Not yet is the world how He would have it. Much of the behaviour that existed then still stalks the land. Corruption, indifference, violence, brutal suppression, crime — you name it, it happens somewhere, sometime.

And humans still seem powerless, in spite of great technological strides, a knowledge explosion and skill in organisation to halt the flood of all that is ugly in human nature.

It would seem then, that His mission was in vain, that His words fell on deaf ears and His example lacked the power to inspire humans to greater endeavours of goodness.

Yet still, He lingers in the minds and imaginations of this present time, just as He has done in the past, just as He will do in the future. He stands as an example in living, as the solution to the problems, the difficulties and the irrational behaviour that plague us today. Not in His fleshly body. That went the way of all flesh — something to be discarded eventually.

Not even in His words, though these carried a message of great importance, but in the living nature, the God He was integrated with. This was His source, His inspiration, His sustenance. This was what He was calling the human race back to — its spiritual homeland where they could join in holy union with the creative power.

Although rejected by many in the land of His birth, over the years His influence has spread and gained considerable attention worldwide. In their hour of need, in times of tribulation, of sorrow and great suffering, people turn to that silent figure, transfixed on the cross, even call His name and pray for His help and guidance.

And in many, a response comes from within, touching the heart, uplifting the mind and giving encouragement and strength to carry on, even spreading gladness and joy where formerly darkness reigned.

Because of this His mission was a worthy one of the utmost value to Mankind and its success is not to be measured by those who fail to respond, but by those who come to that same peace and love He expressed in such a beautiful fashion while He was here.

12

WITH HIS COMING, LOVE
FULFILLED ITS PURPOSE

IT'S THE MAGIC time of Christmas again. Forget the tinsel, the fancy wrapping, the presents, the festivities and the music. These are just the trappings, not the essence.

To get to the real meaning we must journey back to the time when a lone man faced an antagonistic society, without support from family, friends or anyone. Even His closest disciples had turned away. Indeed, one had offered Him to His enemies for a price — 30 pieces of silver is the value recorded in history. How could they value so cheaply the invaluable or put worth on that which is beyond pricing?

Something of great beauty took wings long ago, lifted from the background of suffering and torture; defied the ravages of time, the reasoned debates of mortal people, the rational explanations of the mind, and became established as an unrivalled inspiration for all people to turn to.

He — what He was, what He stood for — refuses to die or fade away. Much as we colour the time in our own fashion, doing what we will in celebration, His coming amongst us was a reminder of how we should live and love, of what we should aspire to.

His actions spoke more eloquently than His words and these were pure distillations of the highest wisdom. He defied all concepts of ordinary human behaviour, rose above the desires of the flesh, the fears and concerns that lurk in the human mind. Even death held no fear for Him.

Such was the stamp of the man and now, again, it's time to honour His life with our usual festivities in one's own way. And to acknowledge, even though here there was a quality life we could never hope to emulate, that a wonder, a mystery, a great depth of love walked amongst us, talked with us, shared itself with us and then left us to our own reflections.

What can one say about a life so beautifully lived, of such impact on the human scene on this planet? He won our hearts if not our minds and the nature of what He was is with us still, calling us back to that strange mystery that inspired His journey amongst us. Oh, if only everyone could share this nature, what a wonderful world it would be.

13

NEVER AGAIN SUCH A SACRIFICE

SOMETHING DARKLY DISTURBING took place almost two thousand years ago. Step by step, events unfolded, till goodness was transfixed on a wooden cross and crucified for the eventual enlightenment of Mankind.

There are many contrasts in life. Night and day, light and shade and here, in this little corner of the Earth, the forces of goodness met the evil side of human nature in a head-on confrontation. A display of the essential nature of each so that all who bore witness could see and determine for themselves the intrinsic worth of what each had to offer. On the surface, the ugly side showed its awesome power backed by authority and blind obedience to tradition.

Goodness, without the backing of physical power and authoritative support, silently acquiesced to the indignities and pain that followed — was lacerated according to the prevailing will then, as an object lesson to others of like intent, paraded before all and sundry until the final barbaric act: aloneness in suffering on the cross.

Long hours of suffering — with thoughts of what? Of agony and pain, torment and discomfort, of whether it was all worthwhile? Did fleeting thoughts of doubt flash through that suffering mind? From high in the air, His pain-filled eyes surveyed the scene below — the barren landscape, the wondering people staring anxiously upwards, the Roman guards. And He waited stoically for the final moments of His mission.

Why did goodness decide on a head-on confrontation to draw attention to the need for humans to turn from their sinful ways? Why the need to torture goodness and subject it to pain and torment in such a disturbingly spectacular manner? Was there no other way?

Other prophets had come, faced difficulties but not in such a gruesome way, nor drawn unto themselves such a vicious and sustained attack by the forces of darkness. Why something so shockingly spectacular? Are we humans so dense, so blind that the spoken and written word and an example in gentle living are not in themselves enough to move us from our stupid ways?

The impact of those times is with us still. And still the forces of darkness have had their way in spite of it all. So much disturbing human behaviour continues right to this very day. And here we are, we still celebrate those events and that life. They have become the cornerstone of the Christian religion.

But we have not changed very much. We have not put aside intolerance, blindness, violent and selfish behaviour and all else that needs to be put aside if we are to join the love that willingly underwent the trials and tribulations that led to the cross of dark suffering — that was, by the resurrection, to be transformed into the inspiring cross of light.

14

AN EASTER REFLECTION

TODAY AS I SIT at my desk to write, it is Good Friday. At this time, Christians commemorate events that happened two thousand years ago. On a day of infamy, humans much like you and me subjected a most gentle and understanding man to torture and forced Him to parade down a crowd-lined path carrying a heavy wooden cross. At Calvary, a place notorious for execution by crucifixion, He was nailed to His cross and raised high into the air. There, He was left to suffer and eventually to die.

Just for good measure, when His body was taken down, a soldier brutally thrust a spear through it. Uncertainty about His death was something the authorities of the day intended to avoid. For prior to the crucifixion there had been a story circulating that area that in the event of His death in such a manner, this man, who claimed He was in harmony with a living God — in fact, one with God — would raise His fleshly body from its grave, out of its state of death and walk and talk again with the living.

Such a resurrection would give authenticity to the man and His teachings. His presence and the things He spoke about were a direct challenge to the civil and religious authorities of the time and, as His popularity grew, so His actions and words were seen as a threat that had to be eradicated.

The story of His trial has come down to us through the Bible. No one took the witness stand and testified on His behalf. Not even His stalwart disciples, who, at the first sign of danger had scattered like rabbits into underground warrens when the jackal is about, prowling for food. Nor any of those whom He had healed from various afflictions of body and mind.

Everyone who could support him was absent, so alone He had to face an invective tide of accusations. Just as He was before the trial — standing alone, talking alone, supported by no one but that God He spoke of in such glowing and inspirational terms.

It is very upsetting to those of us who care about these things that such gentleness and love should be sacrificed on the altar of human ignorance, stupidity and misunderstanding.

People such as Christ when they come amongst us, have no physical protection against the ugly tide of darkness that rails against their saintly presence. Yet, knowing this, still they come, prepared to serve a blighted people with a love and understanding that defies reasonable logic. When common sense demands that they be silent, they speak out, fearlessly so. When the opposition closes in like wolves to devour prey, do they hide or depart? No, they stay.

What is the purpose of it today, to those of us who still debate the meaning of what happened then, with reasonable minds that have neither insights into this man's life, nor in the God that inspired Him?

That series of happenings must have had considerable impact on those who came into contact with them. They are not lightly set in motion, for it could hardly be said that a god of love would enjoy the brutal spectacle of barbaric treatment handed out by a group of humans to a divinely inspired man.

Despite protests that this should not have

been sanctioned from up high, one is left with the uneasy feeling that there was no other way to shock brutal and unfeeling people out of the ugly channels of living they had forged for themselves.

Yet still, there is something that rankles about the whole business. There are many even who question the validity of the records we have of this time, who say that distortion has taken place and that there is no hard, incontrovertible evidence that what is recorded, did so, exactly as it happened. The crucifixion and the resurrection have become the cornerstones of traditional Christianity. They are accepted as evidence of a love and understanding that defies logic and rises above the powerful fear of death. That overrides even the tremendous desire for self-preservation and protection.

Could it be that this was the intention? To confound and disturb an inconsiderate people — to show that there is a love and a God nature that made it possible for the things to be. So that we, in our turn, would be inspired to turn away from ugly and godless directions in living and seek this source for ourselves.

Humans are always drawn to the spectacular and the unusual — unfortunately so. We seem to ignore the ordinary. Notice how we crowd around the healers, the prophets who foretell the future with accuracy, people who have unusual gifts. Even scientists are attracted by strange manifestations.

Is this why it was allowed to happen? That such was the condition of human nature in that time frame and also in the years to follow, that the darkness of human living could only be breached by the coming of Jesus Christ? By His defiance of the traditional religious attitudes of the day, His healing powers? And above all, by the symbol that stands as a stark reminder of the highest love and the brutality of human behaviour – the wooden cross, rearing its shape high above the ground with a silent and compliant figure at the crossing of the beams? Was this the only way to convince the people of that time that there is more to life than the violence, the selfishness and greed that prevailed then and which has continued since, even to this day?

I wonder, but still today it hurts deep down when I reflect on it and today, being Good Friday, it rises anew to disturb me. They had no right or need to do that to Him.

15

AN EASTER INTERLUDE

GOOD FRIDAY. THE day the body of Christ was crucified. Little did the perpetrators know what they were setting in motion. They believed they were protecting their positions of power and authority. Were they not the religious trustees of the day, the guardians of religious traditions? And wasn't all this threatened by this Galilean, this supposed performer of miracles, this healer of the sick? Why, it was even said He raised a man from the dead, brought him back to life before his grieving family and friends.

It's just not possible. The dead are dead. Or

they were in those days without the techniques of modern medicine. Now, with injections of drugs, heart massage, artificial resuscitation and maybe even an electrical charge, it sometimes happens the seemingly dead are brought back to life. In those days it was some feat. So the Galilean became quite a centre of interest wherever He walked, talked and performed His miracles.

What a nuisance He became to the religious authorities of the day. Not intentionally of course. He just went about doing His Father's business (as He so simply put it), dispensing love and truth regardless of the consequences. Perhaps it wouldn't have been so bad if He didn't mention in an offhand way that He and the Father were one. In the eyes of the guardians of the day, this was blasphemy of the highest order.

So, off with His head or, as was the delightful custom in this particular place and time, off to the cross with him. But wait — a whipping first, just to add injury to insult. Mock the man and what He represented, then leave him there, high in the air, exposed to the elements till nature took its course.

The trouble was, after it was all over, He stubbornly refused to stay dead. No. He had to compound the situation by coming back to life, (just as He had forecast, mind you).

And everything about the man, His life, His words, His actions, the miracles, the crucifixion, refused to die away too. In fact, what the priests tried to destroy took on a new lease of life, spread from that centre of a beginning to travel around the world. Much like a tiny seed grows into a mighty oak tree. Which just goes to show that Divine love and truth are irrepressible elements in human nature and in the universe — that they will persist as long as the universe and life persists. And even beyond that, for they have their source in that which is imperishable, in that which is sacred and not profaned. Christ came from that source, was one with it as indeed all things and all life are one with it. All He did was speak the truth and for that He was crucified by the blind, the arrogant and the ignorant.

But the spark that took off then is with us still. It burns like a flame in the hearts of those who travel inwards, who rediscover the Cosmic Christ within. That's what it was all about — to bring Mankind together with truth, love and the Universal Nature. So the cross, instead of signifying the end became a guiding beacon, a signpost for Mankind to rediscover itself, to disentangle itself from its home in time and find its true home in that strange nature beyond space and time.

16

WILL WE SEE HIS LIKE AGAIN?

WHEN THE SPOTLIGHT of religious investigation turns back to almost two thousand years ago, the name that leaps into prominence is that of Jesus Christ. Such was His impact that time before is recorded as BC, that after as AD. All other personalities of the time, whether kings, governors, judges or whatever, merge into a background that points with compelling significance towards this man.

Who was He? Where did He come from? Why is He held in such high esteem? Indeed, His life is held to be the highest example possible in human living. Was it the miracles He is said to have performed — the recorded cases of healing? Was it the deeply inspired sermons, the prayers and the parables that have come down to us? Was it His amazing courage in facing formidable odds, in standing alone without support in His time of tribulation? Was it His unfailing determination to face torture, to endure the cross and subsequent death without compromising His standing or His expression of spiritual truth?

Or was it a combination of all these qualities that together make up the framework of a truly remarkable man, the like of which may never grace this earth again? Such was the depth and nature of His expression that many in the world are still moved to tears by its beauty, gentleness and loving qualities. Although long gone in a physical sense, His name and presence can still move mountains of difficulties, smooth out intractable problems, inspire poems, songs and prose, and artists to higher endeavours, sinners to redemption and all who are touched in some way, to better living.

He bothers the conscience of the human race, still. His image in stone graces many a church across the world. He is adored, praised, worshipped by His admirers and His life is a cause for celebration year after year. He is also scorned, ridiculed and reviled by those who do not understand, who find such a gentle and loving expression with its emphasis in God too much of a threat to the social systems they intend to create and maintain.

Today, His influence is still widespread and a potent force for good. No one can find a shred of factual evidence that points towards corruption, falsehood or erratic behaviour. Nothing that can impugn His character has ever been uncovered. He stands on a spiritual pedestal of greatness, reflecting the qualities of the Divine Strangeness that ever shines within the human race. By the sheer force of love, beauty and truth He conquered the hearts of millions.

His presence is with us still in every act of goodness, in the compassion, love and appreciation of beauty reflected everywhere by humans regardless of race or creed. Jesus Christ, for the support you gave the people of this world in their hour of need, for the love you shared without reservation, for the unbending courage you displayed on the cross, for the truths you shared that will endure forever, I salute you and pay homage with these words I willingly write on your behalf. May you rest content in the heartland of that God you so willingly and wholeheartedly served. On behalf of the human race, my deepest love and admiration.

17

AN OPEN LETTER TO JESUS

DEAR JESUS,
LISTEN mate. About this coming back to straighten up the world. Don't do it. We haven't changed much and you know what happened the last time you were here. Sure, they've done away with the cross. People aren't crucified anymore but they can think of a lot of ways of cutting your next visit short if you make a nuisance of yourself.

Now you know that a lot of powerful interests wouldn't want you around. No way. Take the military command. They can't have you going around saying, "Thou shalt not kill and love your enemies." And you don't carry weapons or use them. That would never do, would it? Love your enemies indeed. Here, they kill as fast as they can. And what about the politicians. Could they have a popular chap like you parading about the place? Just to see large crowds gathering to hear your words — why, it's enough to make a politician green with envy. They'd think up some way of getting you out of the way. Particularly if the cry goes out, "Jesus for world leader." And you with no political party to support you either. Shame on you.

Then there's the rich and famous. You know that saying about a camel going through the eye of a needle before a rich man makes it to Heaven? How many supporters would you collect there? Not many, I grant you. They'd want you out of the way too. You'd make them feel bad.

I think the magicians of the world would also be very upset. You'd soon have a monopoly. They'd insist you joined the magicians' union — on condition you showed them the secret of how it's all done.

Getting worried mate? Let's continue. Now there's the medical profession. They can't have you going around willy nilly, healing here and there, without going through the medical schools, or using medicines and instruments. And without charging, either. That's unheard of. They'd soon go out of business. They'd have you charged with practising without a licence, have you banned and sent off into outer space in a rocket. A one-way trip to nowhere with no return.

Then let's consider the churches. If you didn't support and claim these as your own they would say you were an imposter, a fake, or have you put away for suffering delusions of grandeur. Especially if you come out with you and God are one. They wouldn't burn you at the stake, not these days, but they'd do their best to shut you up and discredit you.

Scientists too couldn't have you around doing some of those amazing things you did last time. Defying the natural order of things like that. They'd slap electrodes all over your body, banks of computers would be tuned in and they wouldn't let you go till they found out how you made it happen.

Psychologists would cluster around with constant questions and examinations. There is no way you could escape the attention. Which brings me to TV. You didn't have this last time around. But it's a fact of life today. You'd be offered a fortune by the various channels, just to have exclusive rights to on-the-spot performances by the one and only original Christ. It would be the show of the century (like it was before). There'd be no peace for you.

So, you get the picture don't you? It wouldn't be worth it. Sure, you'd pick up a few friends here and there. But you'd do that anyway even if you didn't return. You see, we couldn't stand any mistreatment of you the second time around. Not to a guy so gentle, so caring. Leave us to our fate mate, until we've had enough of our ugly ways. Perhaps then, the likes of you can walk this world in freedom, unmolested in any way and get a right good hearing.

That's about it. Merry Christmas. Enjoy yourself wherever you are and God be with you. Oops, a bit of a boo-boo there. That goes without saying. After all, that's what it was all about last time, wasn't it? Affectionately yours,

Joseph Raffa (A spiritual seeker from way back)

18

BEYOND THE CROSS

ONE OF THE most heartrending and inspirational symbols gifted to the human race is that of Jesus nailed to the cross. Such was the impact of that sacrifice that it raised a body of Christians who carried His message outwards in every direction from its centre at Calvary.

That message is with us still. There is Love. There is God. There is redemption. No matter the stains on our character, if we are earnest, if we are sincere, so the mystery of Love, of God, will accept our return without conditions or reservation. Just as we are, we will be accepted, but we return different. Renewed, recharged, washed pure and clean with every stain removed. You just can't beat that kind of love. It was more than humans who nailed Christ to the cross. Love was the power that took him there, that supported frail flesh; that held him there until the symbolic action was completed.

Now, it shines like a lighthouse in the darkness of human suffering. Its inspiration is the light that draws the lost ones to its brightness. In the quality of that love lies the hope of Mankind for a better life. Here is our beacon, given in blood and sacrifice. His pain is our pain. His suffering, ours. His love too, is ours to share.

All we need to do is give over our lives, not as a sacrifice on the cross of torture but willingly, as a gesture of our sincere intention to yield the self in service to a higher cause.

The reverberation from that cross, from that time, has not yet exhausted its wonderful potential for transformation, nor yet reached its culmination — that of raising the human race to the highest level of Being, into the presence of that which is divine. Human nature holds back as yet, drawn to flesh and timeful experience, to security through the mind and its endeavours.

God is still the unknown, still a mystery far removed to human perception. Not yet has it made its presence felt in every human heart nor stirred each human mind into a higher awareness of its nature. It dwells silently within all as the centre of their lives, yet busy minds fail to notice so time-tuned have they become.

Hence the purpose of the cross — a volcanic spiritual outpouring of light and love, centred in the life of Christ. A dramatic demonstration on an earthly stage of the power of God, of the meaning of Love, of the ascendancy of light over darkness.

Whenever people flounder and lose their way, when suffering becomes too much to bear, the cross is the signpost that points to what lies beyond. Climb the meaning of the cross. Discover what lies behind its purpose. There is pure magic in 'that' which sent Christ on a mission of mercy.

Go beyond the symbol, the beauty of the sacrifice, the words that we lose ourselves in; go beyond the actions and the deeds we know to that strange heartland where love alone is. Just go. Lose touch with human nature for a blessed moment and join with God. That is the call of the cross.

Not as a staging post for rest and succour but as an inspirational impulse to travel on until we are lodged, heart and soul in that which is beyond all symbols, beyond all words, beyond all ideas. And here you will meet the Christ you do not know.

19

IN CONCLUSION

THESE DAYS, STORIES go around that seek to drag Christ down to a very human level. There is the denial of His death on the cross, of any miracles whatsoever and attempts to explain away the resurrection. He is said to have married, divorced, had children — all intending to show that Christ was very human and not God-like.

From an unenlightened human standpoint such an intensely inspired, spiritual outpouring is impossible to understand. The radiance, the depth of love, the years spent in service without thought of return or reward — what can we hope to understand without experience of the God-like in ourselves?

The intellect is like a sledgehammer in such delicate matters. Reason is easily perplexed, having only its own experiences as a guide. In the insights and visions that have come my way, a radiant goodness, an incredible aura comes through. Certainly not that of ordinary people, of the likes of you and me. He was the centre of a remarkable outpouring from a higher level of being. Say what we will, we can't take anything away from His high spiritual standing. Such was the force of this outward flow, that after a short incubation period, it gathered strength and in wave after wave, travelled worldwide.

It met and mingled with other, different outpourings. The messages are one and the same regardless of outer diversification in the expressions. There is something grander and greater than what we see and know about ourselves. That the highest purpose in life is to make our way back to this, to integrate, then express this in our surface lives. Call it God, the higher self, Nirvana, enlightenment, the descriptions matter little. Only the discovery counts and the living of it.

That's what Christ came to demonstrate and He did it in style, with courage, endurance and above all, with the greatest love for Mankind.

ABOUT THE AUTHOR

Joseph Raffa was born in 1927 in Fremantle, Western Australia. The second son of Italian immigrants, he enjoyed an idyllic childhood roaming the bush and the seashore with his brothers. In his teens Joseph became a dedicated atheist, looking to science for answers to the riddles of life and the universe. Then, in his early twenties, he experienced a moment of discovery that transformed his life. As Joseph's life opened out spiritually following this awakening, he was inspired to put pen to paper to encourage others to embark on their own journey of discovery. Joseph died of cancer in 2010, leaving behind a legacy of inspirational writing which is now being made available to a wider audience.

For information about Joseph's books and regular blog posts of his spiritual writing, visit www.towardsthesilentheart.com

The Silent Guardian

A timely reminder of our spiritual journey and true purpose on Earth.

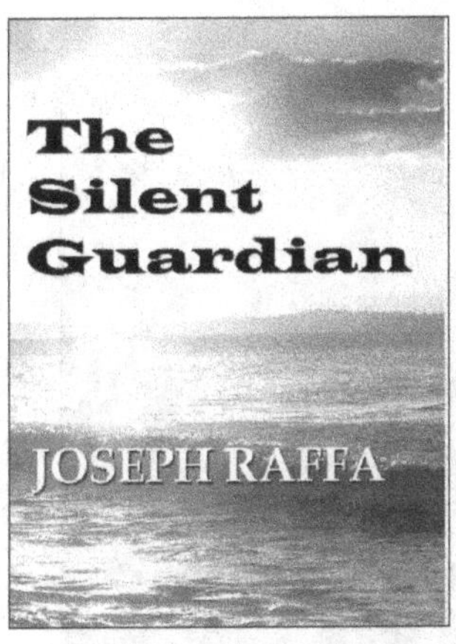

"Explore the planets, the outer reaches of space, the depths of the seas. Burrow into the earth, climb every mountain. When you have seen it all, you will still be left with the mystery of yourself. Turn and face this. Explore this. When you've travelled the extent and depth of the human expression, much of what you learn will be beyond the mind's capacity to convey through verbalisation. When heart speaks to heart, what more is there to say?"

Beside Still Waters

This beautiful collection of essays touches on the universal search for meaning and inspires readers to reach out for the still waters of the spirit.

"The human heart longs for peace and harmony. It seeks a restful haven from the relentless busyness of everyday life, drawing us to spend tranquil moments in natural surrounds that offer a brief respite from the hustle and bustle. There is a state of inner stillness, when the endless chatter of the mind has ceased, that a deeper understanding arises. These are the 'still waters' that bring new life to Mankind, that lay claim to the heart and redirect the mind. These are the waters of peace, love and true togetherness that lift us to divine heights of being and living."